MASTER
WHAT MATTERS

T0382862

MAXWELL MOMENTS

MASTER WHAT MATTERS

12 VALUE CHOICES TO HELP YOU WIN AT LIFE

JOHN C. MAXWELL

CENTER
STREET

Nashville • New York

The author is represented by Yates & Yates, LLP, Literary Agency, Santa Ana, California.

Center Street
Hachette Book Group
1290 Avenue of the Americas, New York, NY 10104
centerstreet.com
twitter.com/centerstreet

First Edition: September 2022

Center Street is a division of Hachette Book Group, Inc. The Center Street name and logo are trademarks of Hachette Book Group, Inc.

The publisher is not responsible for websites (or their content) that are not owned by the publisher.

The Hachette Speakers Bureau provides a wide range of authors for speaking events. To find out more, go to www.HachetteSpeakersBureau.com or call (866) 376-6591.

Print book interior design by Bart Dawson.

Scripture quotations are taken from the Holy Bible, New International Version®, NIV®. Copyright © 1973, 1978, 1984, 2011 by Biblica, Inc.™ Used by permission of Zondervan. All rights reserved worldwide. www.zondervan.com The "NIV" and "New International Version" are trademarks registered in the United States Patent and Trademark Office by Biblica, Inc.™ | Scripture quotations are also taken from THE MESSAGE, copyright © 1993, 2002, 2018 by Eugene H. Peterson. Used by permission of NavPress, represented by Tyndale House Publishers. All rights reserved.

Library of Congress Cataloging-in-Publication Data has been applied for.

ISBNs: 978-1-5460-0250-5 (paperback), 978-1-5460-0251-2 (ebook)

Printed in the United States of America

LSC-C

Printing 1, 2022

CONTENTS

WINNING

AT LIFE

"IF YOU WANT TO BE SUCCESSFUL,
IT'S JUST THIS SIMPLE.
KNOW WHAT YOU ARE DOING.
LOVE WHAT YOU ARE DOING.
AND BELIEVE IN WHAT YOU ARE DOING."

—Will Rogers

HOW DO YOU DEFINE WINNING AT LIFE?

Is it becoming rich?

Is it being famous?

Is it having more friends than you can count?

Is it finding the right life partner?

Is it being great at something?

Is it having the perfect job?

Is it not needing to have a job at all?

What would be a successful life for you?
And how can you get there?

For years I've defined success as:

Knowing your purpose.
Growing to your potential.
Sowing seeds that benefit others.

Does that definition work for you? If so, how can you live that?

By making the right value choices and living them every day!

"MOST PEOPLE DON'T
LEAD THEIR OWN LIVES—
THEY ACCEPT THEIR LIVES."

—John Kotter

The most successful people in life are the ones who settle their value choices early and manage those choices daily. The earlier you settle these choices in your life, and the longer you live them, the greater your potential for success. If you haven't already settled them, then today is the day to do it!

Winning at life is going to bed at night knowing you have done your best and given yourself to the things that matter the most.

"*I TRY TO DO THE RIGHT THING AT THE RIGHT TIME. THEY MAY JUST BE LITTLE THINGS, BUT USUALLY THEY MAKE THE DIFFERENCE BETWEEN WINNING AND LOSING.*"

—Kareem Abdul-Jabbar

What matters most?

The choices you make every day based on your values.

- ☐ Focus on today.
- ☐ See the glass as half-full.
- ☐ View everyone as a potential friend.
- ☐ Do what you say you'll do.
- ☐ Put *important* ahead of *urgent*.
- ☐ Give your family your best.
- ☐ Make yourself better every day.
- ☐ Think your way to the top.
- ☐ Never put off your health.
- ☐ Keep money in perspective.
- ☐ Make room for faith.
- ☐ Give more than you take.

That's my list. Unless you already have a better one, I suggest you begin with this one. Embrace these values and make the choices needed to live them every day, and you will win at life.

Success isn't something you achieve.
***Successful* is something you are.**

"For me, winning isn't something that happens suddenly on the field when the whistle blows and the crowds roar. Winning is something that builds physically and mentally every day that you train and every night that you dream."

—Emmitt Smith

"NICE GUYS MAY APPEAR
TO FINISH LAST, BUT USUALLY
THEY ARE RUNNING
IN A DIFFERENT RACE."

—Ken Blanchard and Norman Vincent Peale

FOCUS

ON

TODAY

Today is the only time you have.

It's too late for yesterday. And you can't depend on tomorrow. You know this. Most people do. But they don't live that way. Their focus is behind them or ahead of them. Neither is helpful. Today is where we need to focus. Today matters. Today is most important. Most of the time, we miss that.

How can you change your mindset?

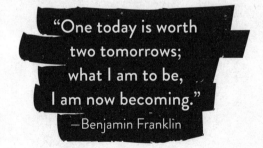

"One today is worth two tomorrows; what I am to be, I am now becoming."
—Benjamin Franklin

"When I was teaching basketball, I urged my players to try their hardest to improve on that very day, to make that practice a masterpiece. Too often we get distracted by what is outside our control. You can't do anything about yesterday. The door to the past has been shut and the key thrown away. You can do nothing about tomorrow. It is yet to come. However, tomorrow is in large part determined by what you do today. So make today a masterpiece...This rule is even more important in life than in basketball."

—John Wooden in *Wooden: A Lifetime of Observations and Reflections on and off the Court*

DON'T OVEREXAGGERATE YESTERDAY

Our past successes and failures often look bigger to us in hindsight than they really were.

Some people never get over their past accomplishments. They'd rather spend time thinking about when they were at the top than trying to reach that level again. Or they regret what they *could have* done. Almost any opportunity that went unpursued looks golden now that it's too late to go after it. Some people's negative experiences shape them for their entire lives.

They relive every rejection, failure, and injury they've received, and they let those incidents tie them into emotional knots.

Yesterday ended last night. No matter how badly you might have failed in the past, it's done. No matter what goals you may have accomplished or awards you may have received, they have little impact on what you do today.

Today is a new day.

DON'T
OVERESTIMATE
TOMORROW

What is your attitude toward the future? What do you expect it to hold? Many people figure that tomorrow is bound to be better, but they have no strategy for *making* it better. In fact, the worse some people feel about today, the more they exaggerate how good tomorrow is likely to be. Don't buy into that lottery mindset.

Hoping for a good future without investing in today is like a farmer waiting for a crop without ever planting any seed.

"Multitudes of people have failed to live for today. They have spent their lives reaching for the future. What they have had within their grasp today they have missed entirely, because only the future has intrigued them...and the first thing they knew the future became the past."

—William Allen White

DON'T
UNDERESTIMATE
TODAY

Have you ever heard someone say, "I'm just killing time"? What a terrible thing to say! Have you ever really thought about that statement? A person might as well say, "I'm throwing away my life" or "I'm killing myself." Benjamin Franklin was right when he said that time is the stuff life is made of.

Today is the only time we have within our grasp. Don't let it slip through your fingers.

"SUCCESS IS PEACE OF MIND, WHICH IS A DIRECT RESULT OF SELF-SATISFACTION IN KNOWING YOU DID YOUR BEST TO BECOME THE BEST THAT YOU ARE CAPABLE OF BECOMING."

—John Wooden

"THE LIFEBUILDER'S CREED"

By Dale Witherington

Today is the most important day of my life.

Yesterday with its successes and victories, struggles and failures

is gone forever.

The past is past.

Done.

Finished.

I cannot relive it. I cannot go back and change it.

But I will learn from it and improve my Today.

Today. This moment. NOW.

It is God's gift to me and it is all that I have.

Tomorrow with all its joys and sorrows,

triumphs and troubles isn't here yet.

Indeed, tomorrow may never come.
Therefore, I will not worry about tomorrow.

Today is what God has entrusted to me.
It is all that I have. I will do my best in it.
I will demonstrate the best of me in it—
my character, giftedness, and abilities—
to my family and friends, clients and associates.
I will identify those things that are most important to do Today
and those things I will do until they are done.
And when this day is done
I will look back with satisfaction at that which I have accomplished.
Then, and only then, will I plan my tomorrow,
Looking to improve upon Today, with God's help.

Then I shall go to sleep in peace…content.

If we want to do something with our lives, then we must focus on today. That's where success lies. But how do you win today? How do you make today a great day instead of one that falls to pieces? Here's the missing piece: The secret of your success is determined by your daily agenda.

If you would change your life, focus on today.

"THE GREATEST GAP IN LIFE
IS THE ONE BETWEEN
KNOWING AND DOING."

—Dick Biggs

SEE THE GLASS AS HALF-FULL

NO ONE HAS
A PERFECT LIFE

No person's life is a full glass. No person's life is an empty glass. Every day of your life, the glass has something positive in it. When you look at the glass of your life, what do you see?

Seeing the glass as half-full increases your possibilities. Pessimists usually get what they expect. So do optimists.

Believing in yourself increases your chances of success.

Looking for the positive in every situation helps you see opportunities you would otherwise miss.

Being positive with people prompts them to be positive with you—and individuals who interact well with others have a leg up on people who don't.

I can't think of one legitimate criticism of being positive. **It's all good.**

GET AHEAD OF
THE GAME

In today's competitive culture, everybody is looking for an edge. **Possessing a positive attitude is like having a secret weapon.**

There are things in your life that you cannot choose: your parents, where you were born, your height, your race, your natural talents. But you can always choose your outlook. If you want to have a better day, a better year, a better life, then you need to see the world positively.

"THINGS TURN OUT BEST FOR THE PEOPLE WHO MAKE THE BEST OF THE WAY THINGS TURN OUT."

—John Wooden

"NOTHING CAN STOP THE MAN
WITH THE RIGHT MENTAL ATTITUDE
FROM ACHIEVING HIS GOAL;
NOTHING ON EARTH CAN
HELP THE MAN WITH
THE WRONG MENTAL ATTITUDE."

—Thomas Jefferson

The thoughts in your mind will always be more important than the things in your life. Fame and fortune are fleeting. The satisfaction that comes from achievement is momentary. Solomon, the wisest of all kings, observed, "He who loves silver will not be satisfied with silver; nor he who loves abundance, with increase."

You cannot buy or win happiness.
You must choose it.

"He who has so little knowledge of human nature as to seek happiness by changing anything but his own disposition will waste his life in fruitless efforts and multiply the grief which he purposes to remove."

—Samuel Johnson

"PRAYER FOR THE RIGHT OUTLOOK"

Author Unknown

Dear Lord,

So far today, I am doing alright. I have not gossiped,
lost my temper, been greedy, grumpy, nasty, selfish, or
self-indulgent. I have not whined, cursed, or eaten
any chocolate.

However, I am going to get out of bed in a few minutes,
and I will need a lot more help after that.

Amen.

CHANGE YOUR THINKING

If you want to see the glass as half-full, but haven't done so in the past, then change your mind. That's something you *can* choose to do. Believe you can be positive, that you can change into the person you desire to be. **If your thinking changes, then everything else can follow.**

"WHAT LIES BEHIND US
AND WHAT LIES BEFORE US
ARE TINY MATTERS COMPARED
TO WHAT LIES WITHIN US."

—Ralph Waldo Emerson

CHANGE YOUR WORDS

After you change how you think, change what you say...

If you continually look for and embrace the positive, you'll help yourself live more positively every day.

ELIMINATE THESE WORDS

I can't

I don't think

I won't have the time

I'm afraid

I don't believe

SAY THESE INSTEAD

I can

I think

I will make the time

I'm confident

I'm sure

CHANGE YOUR LEVEL OF GRATITUDE

Remaining grateful will help you to see the half-full glass.

It will make you more positive. And having a positive attitude helps you to think more about the good rather than the bad. It's a positive cycle that helps to fuel itself.

Seeing the glass as half-full
will not change your circumstances.

But it will change your life. You will still have challenges, but you will know you can face them. You will deal with tragedies, but you will possess hope for weathering them. You will get knocked down, but you will be able to get back up. When the sun comes up, you will be grateful. When the stars come out, you will be hopeful. No matter what life brings, you will see the good, and you will be able to smile.

"When we learn to give thanks, we are learning to concentrate not on the bad things, but on the good things in our lives."

—Amy Vanderbilt

VIEW EVERYONE AS A POTENTIAL FRIEND

When you understand people
and care about them, you're less likely
to take their shortcomings personally.
And you lay the groundwork
for better relationships.

Think back to the most important experiences of your life: the highest highs, the greatest victories, the most daunting obstacles overcome. How many of them happened to you alone? I bet there are very few. When you understand that being connected to others is one of life's greatest joys, then you realize that the best of life comes when you initiate and invest in good relationships.

What's the best way to develop relationships with others?

**Start off by seeing *everyone*
as a potential friend.**

HELLO, FRIEND!

The best way to start off on the right foot with people is to put others first. The most basic way to do that is to practice the Golden Rule: Do unto others as you would have them do unto you. If you take that mindset into all your interactions with others, you can't go wrong.

But there are other ways to show people they matter and that you are interested in their well-being: taking time to meet people, remembering people's names, smiling at everyone, and being quick to offer help. **People don't care how much you know until they know how much you care.**

BE A FRIEND

There's an old saying in sales: all things being equal, the likeable person wins. But all things not being equal, the likeable person still wins. There's no substitute for relational skill when it comes to getting ahead in any aspect of life. **People who alienate others have a hard time.**

When people don't like you...they'll try to hurt you.

If they can't hurt you...they won't help you.

If they *have* to help you...they won't hope you succeed.

When they hope you don't succeed...life's victories feel hollow.

"RELATIONSHIPS HELP US TO DEFINE WHO WE ARE AND WHAT WE CAN BECOME. MOST OF US CAN TRACE OUR SUCCESSES TO PIVOTAL RELATIONSHIPS."

—Donald O. Clifton and Paula Nelson

HAVE A HEART FOR PEOPLE

To succeed in life, you must care about people.
Expect the best from everyone. Assume people's motives are good
unless they prove you wrong. Value people according to their
best moments.

**Offer people your friendship rather than asking
for theirs.** Friendship will ultimately be their decision.
When you like people and have a heart for them, no matter
where you go, you'll meet a friend.

"YOU CAN'T MAKE THE OTHER
FELLOW FEEL IMPORTANT
IN YOUR PRESENCE IF YOU
SECRETLY FEEL
THAT HE IS A NOBODY."

—Les Giblin

MAKE UNDERSTANDING OTHERS YOUR GOAL

When you desire to improve your understanding of people, you open the door to positive relationships. As you interact with others, work to bridge the gap of understanding:

- ☐ People can be insecure—give them confidence.
- ☐ People want to feel special—sincerely compliment them.
- ☐ People desire a better tomorrow—show them hope.
- ☐ People need to be understood—listen to them.
- ☐ People can be selfish—speak to their needs first.
- ☐ People get emotionally low—encourage them.
- ☐ People want to be associated with success—help them win.

"CARVE YOUR NAME
ON HEARTS AND NOT
ON MARBLE."

—Charles Spurgeon

"Natural talent, intelligence,
a wonderful education—
none of these guarantees success.
Something else is needed:
the sensitivity to understand
what other people want and the
willingness to give it to them."

—John Luther

GIVE RESPECT BUT EXPECT TO EARN IT FROM OTHERS

Every human being deserves to be treated with respect.
By giving people respect first, you lay the foundation for a good relationship. But you can't demand respect. You must earn it. If you respect yourself, respect others, and exhibit competence, others will give you respect.

ADD VALUE TO OTHERS WITH NO EXPECTATION OF RETURN

Some people approach every interaction with others as a transaction. They're willing to add value, but only if they expect to receive value in return. If you want to make friendships possible and relationships a priority, you must check your motives to be sure you are not trying to manipulate others for your own gain.

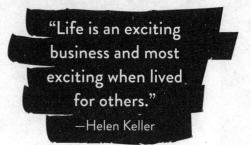

"Life is an exciting business and most exciting when lived for others."

—Helen Keller

"Always start a relationship by asking:
Do I have ulterior motives for wanting
to relate to this person?
Is my caring conditional?
Am I trying to escape something?
Am I planning to change the person?
Do I need this person to help me
make up for a deficiency in myself?
If your answer to any of these questions
is 'yes,' leave the person alone.
He or she is better off without you."

—Leo Buscaglia

Making friends takes effort.

You must be willing to give more than you expect to receive, love others unconditionally, look for ways to add value to others, and bring joy to others. At the end of each day, ask yourself, "Have I been thoughtful toward people today? Would they express joy that they have spent time with me? Have I treated others as potential friends? If the answers are yes, then you've done your part.

DO WHAT YOU SAY YOU'LL DO

"Nothing is easier than
saying words.
Nothing is harder than living them,
day after day.
What you promise today
must be renewed and redecided
tomorrow and each day
that stretches out before you."

—Arthur Gordon

How valuable is following through for winning at life?

When you say you will do something, small or large, do you do it? When you make a commitment, can others be sure you will keep it?

Few value choices have a greater impact than keeping commitments. As much as it helps the recipients of the commitment, it does even more for the person who keeps it.

FOCUS ON CHOICES, NOT CONDITIONS

In general, people approach daily commitment in one of two ways: They focus on the external or the internal. Those who focus on the external allow conditions to determine whether they do what they say they will do. Because conditions are so transitory, their commitment level changes like the wind.

In contrast, people who base their actions on the internal focus on their choices. **Each choice is a crossroads, one that will either confirm or compromise their commitments.**

When you come to a crossroads, you can recognize it because:

- A personal decision is required,
- The decision will cost you something, and
- Others will likely be influenced by it.

Your choices are the only thing you truly control.

You cannot control your circumstances, nor can you control others. By focusing on your choices, and then making them with integrity, you control your commitment. And that is what often separates success from failure.

Anything worth doing is going to be a struggle.

Commitment doesn't come easily, but when you're fighting for something you believe in, the struggle is worth it.

DON'T RELY ON TALENT ALONE

The more talented you are, the more tempted you will be to rely on your talent. If you want to win at life, you need to reach your potential. To reach your potential, you need to add a strong work ethic to your talent.

Your talent is what God put in you before you were born. Your skills are what you put in yesterday. **Commitment is what you must put in today to be successful.**

"The heights by great men
reached and kept
Were not attained by sudden flight,
But they, while their
companions slept,
Were toiling upward in the night."

—Henry Wadsworth Longfellow

"YOU HAVE TO PAY THE PRICE.
YOU WILL FIND THAT EVERYTHING
IN LIFE EXACTS A PRICE,
AND YOU WILL HAVE TO DECIDE
WHETHER THE PRICE
IS WORTH THE PRIZE."

—Sam Nunn

NEVER UNDERVALUE PERSEVERANCE

Nothing stokes commitment like single-minded effort that results in achievement. The turtle often beats the hare if the race is long enough.

> "Anything beyond this will be too much. I can plod. That is my only genius. I can persevere in any definite pursuit. To this I owe everything."
>
> —William Carey

"The moment one definitely commits oneself, then Providence moves too. All sorts of things occur to help one that would never otherwise have occurred. A whole stream of events issue from the decision, raising in one's favor all manner of unforeseen incidents and meetings and material assistance which no man could have dreamed would come his way."

—William H. Murray

WIN THE INTERNAL BATTLE FIRST

When Olympic athletes come into the stadium during the opening ceremonies and prepare to participate in the games, one of the things they do is recite the following:

> **I have prepared.**
> **I have followed the rules.**
> **I will not quit.**

When you agree to do something and you show up to follow through, if you can say those same three sentences, you can be proud no matter what the outcome is.

"PEOPLE FORGET HOW
FAST YOU DID A JOB—
BUT THEY REMEMBER
HOW WELL YOU DID IT."

—Howard W. Newton

"To bring one's self to a frame of mind and to the proper energy to accomplish things that require plain hard work continuously is the one big battle that everyone has. When this battle is won for all time, then everything is easy."

—Thomas A. Buckner

DO WHAT'S RIGHT WHEN YOU DON'T FEEL LIKE IT

If you do what you should only when you feel like it, you won't keep your commitments consistently. You won't do what you say you'll do.

If you refuse to give in to excuses, no matter how good they may sound or how good they will make you feel in the moment, you have the potential to go far.

> "When you're committed to something, you accept no excuses, only results."
>
> —Ken Blanchard

"ALWAYS BEAR IN MIND
THAT YOUR OWN RESOLUTION
TO SUCCESS IS MORE IMPORTANT
THAN ANY OTHER THING."

—Abraham Lincoln

PUT IMPORTANT AHEAD OF URGENT

"Guard well your spare moments. They are like uncut diamonds. Discard them and their value will never be known. Improve them and they will become the brightest gems in a useful life."

—Ralph Waldo Emerson

Given the choice, would you rather save time or money? Most people focus on dollars. But how you spend your time is much more important than how you spend your money. Money mistakes can often be corrected, but when you lose time, it's gone forever. **Your time is priceless.**

YOU CANNOT CONTROL TIME

Have you ever found yourself thinking, "I need more time"?
Well, you're not going to get it! No one gets more time. There are
1,440 minutes in a day. **No matter what you do, you won't
get more.**

Since you can't change time, you must instead change your
approach to it. Most people are driven by the urgent, by whatever
comes up next. To win at life, you can't do that.

"Time management has nothing to do with the clock, but everything to do with organizing and controlling your participation in certain events that coordinate with the clock. Einstein understood time management is an oxymoron. It cannot be managed. You can't save time, lose time, turn back the hands of time or have more time tomorrow than today. Time is unemotional, uncontrolled, unencumbered. It moves forward regardless of circumstances and, in the game of life, creates a level playing field for everyone."

—Myers Barnes

YOU CANNOT DO EVERYTHING

You can work to have *anything* you want, but you can't have *everything* you want. You must choose. Excellence comes from doing the right things right, the important things before the urgent ones. The rest you have to let go of. If you're not sure what the right things are, pretend you have a week to live. What would you do? A month? Six months? **The things you would do in that short time are the right things.**

"BESIDES THE NOBLE ART
OF GETTING THINGS DONE,
THERE IS THE NOBLE ART
OF LEAVING THINGS UNDONE.
THE WISDOM OF LIFE CONSISTS OF THE
ELIMINATION OF NONESSENTIALS."

—Lin Yutang

"DEVOTING A LITTLE OF YOURSELF
TO EVERYTHING MEANS
COMMITTING A GREAT DEAL
OF YOURSELF TO NOTHING."

—Michael LeBoeuf

YOU CHOOSE YOUR LIFE BY HOW YOU SPEND TIME

Everything you are doing now is something you have chosen to do. Maybe you don't want to believe that. But if you're over age twenty-one, your life is what you're making of it. **To change your life, you need to change your priorities.**

"The reason most goals are not achieved is that we spend our time doing second things first."
—Robert J. McKain

WHAT'S IMPORTANT?

Let's face it—there are a lot of things vying for your attention. Many people want to put you on their agenda. Thousands of manufacturers want you to spend your money on their products. Even your own desires can be so diverse and your attention so scattered that you often aren't sure what should get your attention. That's why you need to choose your priorities intentionally.

Ask yourself three questions:

- **What is *required* of you?** What must be done that *only you* can do? In your career, what must you do personally? If you're a leader, that list should be very short. As a spouse or parent, what must you do that should not be left undone? Or that no other person can or should do? These are your most important tasks.

- **What gives you the greatest *return*?** There are certain things you were born to do. They play to your gifts, talents, experience, and opportunities. They constitute your greatest contribution to the world. What are they? These are the next in importance.

- **What gives you the greatest *reward*?** Some tasks or activities make you glad you're alive. They make a difference. They give you a deep sense of satisfaction when you do them. These are also important.

All other tasks are unimportant, and you should work your way out of doing them.

"THE ART OF BEING WISE
IS THE ART OF KNOWING
WHAT TO OVERLOOK."

—William James

To be successful, you can't allow what's urgent for others to drive your life. You can't just run on the fast track. You must run on *your* track. You must choose. When you take control of your day, you take control of your life. It's the only one you get.

Make the most of it.

GIVE YOUR FAMILY YOUR BEST

"When you have a strong family life, you receive the message that you are loved, cared for, and important. The positive intake of love, affection and respect...gives you inner resources to deal with life more successfully."

—Nick Stinnett

YOU CAN'T CHANGE YOUR FAMILY OF ORIGIN

The family of your upbringing formed you, for better or worse. It may have given you a head start in life, or it may have presented you with challenges. You have no control over the past or how you were treated. But you determine how *you* treat *your* family today and in the future.

YOU CAN CHANGE YOUR FAMILY NOW

The way you approach family life has a profound impact on how you live and on the legacy you leave. At its best, a family is:

- A safe haven in a storm
- A photo album of great memories
- A crucible of good character
- A mirror revealing truth
- A treasure chest of our most important relationships

The relationships you have with your spouse, children, parents, and siblings are the most important ones in your life. They form you and are formed by you. **That's reason enough to give them your best.**

Do you want to change the world and make it
a better place? Good.

Start by going home and loving your own family.
Let change begin there.

EXPRESS APPRECIATION FOR EACH OTHER

How do you treat your family moment to moment, day to day? Do you tell them you love them? Do you stop and take time to speak life-giving words to them? You should.

If the members of your family don't receive affirmation and appreciation at home, there's a good chance they won't get it anywhere. Why? Because in general, the world does not give those things to people.

One of the most positive things you can do is tell others you love them simply because they are yours.

"IN EVERY PERSON FROM THE CRADLE TO THE GRAVE, THERE IS A DEEP CRAVING TO BE APPRECIATED."

—William James

RESOLVE CONFLICT AS QUICKLY AS POSSIBLE

When you experience conflict at home, how do you deal with it? A family's response to problems will either bring it together or tear it apart.

Resolve conflict quickly and effectively, and you bring healing. Don't neglect it; otherwise, you may find yourself agreeing with novelist F. Scott Fitzgerald, who said, "Family quarrels are bitter things. They don't go according to any rules. They're not like aches or wounds, they're more like splits in the skin that won't heal because there's not enough material."

You can choose to give your family your best, so that it doesn't have to be that way.

PUT YOUR FAMILY ON YOUR CALENDAR FIRST

Work can gobble up every bit of your time if you let it.
So can hobbies or other interests. If you don't create boundaries for how you spend your time, your family will always get the leftovers.

You can battle that trend by putting your family in your calendar first. Block out time for family vacations months ahead. If you're married, schedule regular frequent time with your spouse. If you have children or grandchildren, prioritize attending their events and simply being with them.

Someone once said that you should never let yourself feel that you ought to be at work when you're with your family, and you should never feel that you ought to be with your family when you're at work.

That's a great goal that comes from the right perspective. But you can achieve it only if you give your family your best.

FIND WAYS TO SPEND TIME TOGETHER

There is no substitute for time when it comes to your family. Since everybody's busy, single-parent households are so common, and in the majority of two-parent families, both parents work, you have to figure out ways to spend time together.

If you're in the midst of raising children, you may need to put your own hobbies on hold. Schedule one-on-one time with each person. And fight for times of fun. Don't let time with family feel like an interruption. Make it an intentional act.

"Time is like oxygen—there's a minimum amount that's necessary for survival. And it takes quantity as well as quality to develop warm and caring relationships."

—Armand Nicholi

CREATE AND MAINTAIN FAMILY TRADITIONS

Family members don't remember most of the gifts they've received for Christmas or on their birthdays. A few items might stand out, but most are forgettable. What do people remember? Great time spent together.

Traditions give your family a shared history and a strong sense of identity. Do you possess good memories of how your family celebrated Thanksgiving when you were a child? How about Christmas or Hanukkah? The traditions your family kept helped define your identity.

Choose to create meaningful traditions during the holidays.

Carry over the things you loved. Make the effort to mark milestones and celebrate rites of passage in your family. Base them on your values and make them your own.

If you can protect and nurture your family,
no matter what else happens in your life,
you—and those you love—
will have a safe place to land.

"The home...is the lens through which we get our first look at marriage and all civic duties; it is the clinic where, by conversation and attitude, impressions are created with respect to sobriety and reverence; it is the school where lessons of truth or falsehood, honesty or deceit are learned; it is the mold which ultimately determines the structure of society."

—Perry F. Webb

MAKE

YOURSELF

BETTER

EVERY DAY

"TO BE WHAT WE ARE,
AND TO BECOME WHAT
WE ARE CAPABLE OF BECOMING,
IS THE ONLY END OF LIFE."

—Robert Louis Stevenson

When we're young, adults, such as our parents and teachers, challenge us to grow. As adults, if we don't take proactive responsibility for our mental, emotional, and professional growth, we lag behind.

Personal growth works exactly opposite to compounding interest in a bank account. If someone deposited a sum of money into an interest-bearing account the day you were born, the way to make it grow would be to leave it alone. But leaving your potential alone won't help you grow. You *must* take it out every day and work with it. That's the only way to keep growing and improving.

A person who believes that growth comes simply as the result of living is like an archer who keeps shooting arrows off target and believes he's improving by shooting the same way. **Experience is good only if it's reflected upon and you learn from both mistakes and successes.**

"When an archer misses
the mark he turns and looks
for the fault within himself.
Failure to hit the bull's-eye
is never the fault of the target.
To improve your aim,
improve yourself."

—Gilbert Arland

WHAT IS YOUR POTENTIAL?

The greatest handicap a person has is not realizing their potential. What dreams do you have that are just waiting to be fulfilled? What gifts and talents are inside you that are dying to be drawn out and developed? **The gap between your vision and your present reality can be filled only through a commitment to maximizing your potential.**

"HELL BEGINS ON THAT DAY WHEN GOD GRANTS US A CLEAR VISION OF ALL THAT WE MIGHT HAVE ACHIEVED, OF ALL THE GIFTS WE WASTED, OF ALL THAT WE MIGHT HAVE DONE THAT WE DID NOT DO."

—Gian Carlo Menotti

FOCUS YOUR GROWTH

As you plan your growth, it will benefit you greatly to be focused. What are your greatest strengths? How are they related to your greatest potential? This is where you need to focus your growth.

Pick your main areas of growth. Then:

☐ Listen to podcasts every week.

☐ Read two or more books on the subject every month.

☐ Meet with an expert to ask questions every quarter.

☐ Take notes and file what you learn every day so you can revisit it.

"The great mystery isn't that people do things badly but that they occasionally do a few things well. The only thing that is universal is incompetence. Strength is always specific. Nobody ever commented, for example, that the great violinist Jascha Heifetz probably couldn't play the trumpet very well."

—Peter Drucker

"IF A PERSON WILL SPEND
ONE HOUR A DAY ON THE SAME
SUBJECT FOR FIVE YEARS,
THAT PERSON WILL BE
AN EXPERT ON THAT SUBJECT."

—Earl Nightingale

EXTERNAL BREAKTHROUGH COMES FROM INTERNAL GROWTH

Have you ever felt like you were just stuck in some aspect of your life? You want to advance in your career, but you seem to have stalled. You desire to improve a relationship, but you aren't able to break new ground. Or you hit a plateau in your health or fitness and nothing you do seems to advance your efforts. How do you overcome such stagnation?

Most people make external changes. They look for a different job, seek a new relationship, or try a crash diet. The problem is that external changes generally only relieve symptoms of difficulties that are internal.

Personal growth changes you from the inside out.

When you improve your career skills, you become better equipped to face challenges. When you learn new emotional and relational skills, you are able to work through relational issues. When you develop habits and disciplines related to eating and exercise, your health and fitness improve.

The way forward starts with internal personal growth.

MAKE IT YOUR GOAL TO GROW IN SOME WAY EVERY DAY

The Tatar tribes of central Asia used this curse against their enemies: "May you stay in one place forever."

If you don't try to improve yourself every day, that could be your fate. You will be stuck in the same place, doing the same things, hoping the same hopes for the future, but never gaining new territory or winning new victories.

"IN ORDER TO DO MORE,
I'VE GOT TO BE MORE."

—Jim Rohn

ENJOY THE JOURNEY

B. Eugene Griessman, author of *Path to High Achievement*, says that it takes most grand masters of chess fifteen years of learning before they win their first world title. That's a fifth of most people's lives.

If you're going to spend that much time learning something, then you had better decide to like it.
If your destination appeals to you, but you cannot enjoy the journey it will take to get there, then you would be wise to reexamine your priorities to make sure you have them right.

"THE ONLY THRILL WORTHWHILE
IS THE ONE THAT COMES
FROM MAKING SOMETHING
OUT OF YOURSELF."

—William Feather

THINK YOUR WAY TO THE TOP

"THOUGHT IS THE ORIGINAL SOURCE OF ALL WEALTH, ALL SUCCESS, ALL MATERIAL GAIN, ALL GREAT DISCOVERIES AND INVENTIONS, AND ALL ACHIEVEMENT."

—Claude M. Bristol

What kind of value do you put on good thinking? Has it been a priority in your life? It doesn't matter what profession you pursue; thinking precedes achievement. Success doesn't come by accident. People don't repeatedly stumble into achievement and then figure it out afterward. Whether you're a doctor, businessperson, carpenter, teacher, parent, or student, your level of success will increase dramatically if you place high value on thinking. The greater your thinking, the greater your potential. **People who are successful at life think their way to the top.**

"A small man is made up of small thoughts."
—Victor Hugo

DON'T BECOME
A SLAVE TO YOUR
SURROUNDINGS

People who do not practice and develop good thinking often find themselves at the mercy of their circumstances. They are unable to solve problems, and they find themselves facing the same obstacles repeatedly. Because they don't think ahead, they are habitually in reaction mode.

Good thinkers can always overcome difficulties, including lack of resources. Poor thinkers are frequently at the mercy of good thinkers.

"BETTER AN EMPTY PURSE
THAN AN EMPTY HEAD."

—German proverb

THE MVP IS THE MVT

Who has the greatest value to any organization?
The person with the ideas!

Ideas are what the United States was founded on. Ideas have helped to create great companies and drive the largest economy in the world. Ideas are the foundation for everything we build, every advance we make. When a person is a good thinker and has lots of ideas, he or she becomes very valuable. If you're a good thinker, you have a great advantage.

Gerald Nadler, author of *Breakthrough Thinking*, says, "Only 10 percent to 12 percent of all managers are effective enough to make and stay on the fast track." Why? They don't mentally stay in the game.

"WHAT IS IMPORTANT IS IDEAS. IF YOU HAVE IDEAS, YOU HAVE THE MAIN ASSET YOU NEED, AND THERE ISN'T ANY LIMIT TO WHAT YOU CAN DO WITH YOUR BUSINESS AND YOUR LIFE."

—Harvey Firestone

IDENTIFY A PLACE, TIME, AND PROCESS FOR THINKING

Find a place where you like to think. Some people like being connected to nature. Others want to be in the midst of—but removed from—activity. J. K. Rowling, author of the Harry Potter books, wrote her first book while sitting in a café. Others like a quiet room, or a view. Where you go doesn't matter, as long as it stimulates your thinking.

Once you have a place, carve out a regular time. Try to discover the time of day when your thinking is the sharpest. Are you a morning person? A night owl? Whenever you're at your best, set aside a block of time every day just to think. You'll find that you're much more productive and focused as a result.

And find a thinking process that works for you.
Poet Rudyard Kipling had to have pure black ink for his pen before he could write. Philosopher Immanuel Kant used to stare out of his window at a stone tower. When trees grew, threatening his view, he chopped them down. Composer Ludwig van Beethoven poured cold water over his head to refresh himself and stimulate his thinking. Poet and lexicographer Samuel Johnson said that he needed a purring cat, an orange peel, and a cup of tea in order to write. Composer Gioachino Rossini felt that he worked best in bed under the covers. **Do whatever works for you.**

NOBODY STARTS AS A GREAT THINKER

If you want to become a great thinker, you first need to become a good thinker. Before becoming a good thinker, you need to become a thinker. In order to become a thinker, you need to be willing to first produce a bunch of mediocre and downright bad ideas. Only by practicing and developing your thinking daily will your ideas get better. Your thinking ability is determined not by your desire to think, but by your past thinking. To become a good thinker, do more thinking. Once the ideas start flowing, they get better. **Once they get better, they keep improving.**

"For me, when an idea hits me, it strikes fire, almost like God speaking. I know that sounds heretical, but there it is. The more time that passes after the idea strikes, the less heat it gives off. I forget parts of it, it doesn't seem as great. Ideas have a short half-life."

—Dave Goetz

DON'T LET GOOD THINKING PREVENT GOOD ACTION

Just because you need to take more time thinking doesn't mean you should take less action. When you have a great idea but don't do anything with it, then you don't reap the advantage that it brings.

Have you ever had an idea for a product or service and a few months or years later seen someone else with the same idea take it to market? Author Alfred Armand Montapert said, "Every time a person puts an idea across, he finds ten people who thought about it *before* he did—but they only *thought* about it."

The ultimate goal of thinking is translating ideas into action. Good thinkers who don't act are smart but unsuccessful. Bad thinkers who do act get themselves and others into trouble.

Good thinkers who take action work their way to the top.

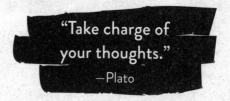

"Take charge of your thoughts."
—Plato

NEVER PUT OFF YOUR HEALTH

"THE GREATEST OF FOLLIES
IS TO SACRIFICE HEALTH
FOR ANY OTHER KIND
OF HAPPINESS."

—Arthur Schopenhauer

**If you want to win at life,
you must make your health a priority.**

This may seem obvious, yet many people
put off good health decisions.

YOUR HEALTH IMPACTS YOU EMOTIONALLY, INTELLECTUALLY, AND SPIRITUALLY

You can escape from a lot of things that might hurt you. You can quit a hazardous job. You can move to a safer location. You can stay away from someone who wants to harm you. But you can't get away from your body. For as long as you live, you're stuck with it. **If you make unhealthy choices, it will affect every aspect of your life—your heart, mind, and spirit.**

"IF I HAD KNOWN
I WAS GOING TO LIVE THIS LONG,
I WOULD HAVE TAKEN
BETTER CARE OF MYSELF."

—attributed to Mickey Mantle

IT'S EASIER TO MAINTAIN GOOD HEALTH THAN TO REGAIN IT

People are funny. When they are young, they will spend their health to get wealth. Later they will gladly pay all they have trying to get their health back.

> "A person too busy to take care of his health is like a mechanic too busy to take care of his tools."
>
> —Spanish proverb

PURPOSE HELPS YOUR HEALTH

Nothing is better than perspective for helping a person want to do the right thing. When you have something to live for, not only does it make you desire a long life, but it also helps you see the importance of the steps along the way.

Seeing the big picture enables you to put up with life's irritations. It's hard to find motivation in the moment when there is no hope in the future. A sense of purpose helps you make decisions to change and then follow through with the discipline required to make that change permanent.

"GIVE A MAN HEALTH
AND A COURSE TO STEER,
AND HE'LL NEVER STOP TO
TROUBLE ABOUT WHETHER
HE'S HAPPY OR NOT."

—George Bernard Shaw

HANDLE STRESS EFFECTIVELY

A hundred years ago, most causes of illness were related to infectious disease. Today they are related to stress. The worst thing you can do when it comes to any kind of potential pressure situation is to put off dealing with it. If you address issues as quickly as possible and keep short accounts with people, you greatly reduce the chances of being stressed-out.

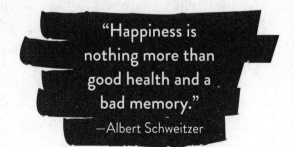

"Happiness is nothing more than good health and a bad memory."
—Albert Schweitzer

DO WORK YOU ENJOY

One of the greatest causes of debilitating stress in people's lives is doing jobs they don't like.

Many people deal with two major frustrations: The first is doing work that they don't think is important. If you do work that you believe adds no value to yourself or anyone else, you quickly become demoralized.

The second is doing jobs that keep them in an area of weakness. You can't work in weak areas and be successful. You must work within your strengths. How do you know when you are doing that? Your work actually gives you energy.

"THE PROBLEM WITH
THE RAT RACE IS THAT
EVEN IF YOU WIN,
YOU'RE STILL A RAT."

—Lily Tomlin

ACCEPT YOUR PERSONAL WORTH

One of the most prolific and successful songwriters of the twentieth century was Irving Berlin. Among the hundreds of songs he wrote were hits such as "God Bless America," "White Christmas," "Easter Parade," "Puttin' On the Ritz," and "There's No Business Like Show Business." In an interview with Berlin in the *San Diego Union-Tribune*, Don Freeman asked the songwriter whether there was a question he had never been asked but that he wished someone would. Berlin replied, "Yes, there is one. 'What do you think of the many songs you've written that didn't become hits?' My reply would be that I *still* think they are wonderful!"

Berlin had a good sense of self-worth and confidence in his work. Maybe that's one of the reasons he lived to be a hundred and one!

Take care of your health, but don't take yourself too seriously.

"AN INDIVIDUAL'S SELF-CONCEPT AFFECTS EVERY ASPECT OF HUMAN BEHAVIOR...IT IS NO EXAGGERATION TO SAY THAT A STRONG POSITIVE SELF-IMAGE IS THE BEST POSSIBLE PREPARATION FOR SUCCESS IN LIFE."

—Dr. Joyce Brothers

"I've done the research
and I hate to tell you,
but everybody dies—lovers, joggers,
vegetarians and non-smokers.
I'm telling you this so that some
of you who jog at 5 a.m.
and eat vegetables will occasionally
sleep late and have an ice cream cone."

—Bernie S. Siegel in *Peace, Love and Healing*

LAUGH

Don't take life too seriously. And certainly don't take yourself too seriously. Everyone has idiosyncrasies. Don't let yours bother you. They can cause you to despair or to laugh. If you can laugh at yourself loudly and often, you will find it liberating. There's no better way to prevent stress from becoming distress.

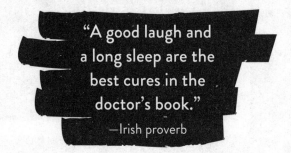

"A good laugh and a long sleep are the best cures in the doctor's book."
—Irish proverb

EAT RIGHT
AND EXERCISE

Do I really need to write anything here? If you're overweight, you already know what to do. Eat fewer calories than you burn. Exercise every day. Drink water.

Most people's problem isn't knowledge. It's action.

> "The only way to keep your health is to eat what you don't want, drink what you don't like, and do what you'd rather not."
> —Mark Twain

KEEP MONEY IN PERSPECTIVE

"THE AVERAGE AMERICAN
IS BUSY BUYING THINGS
HE DOESN'T WANT WITH
MONEY HE DOESN'T HAVE
TO IMPRESS PEOPLE
HE DOESN'T LIKE."

—O. Donald Olson

People tend to value money and things over what's really important in life: other people.
French historian and political scientist Alexis de Tocqueville remarked about the United States that he knew of "no other country where love of money has such a grip on men's hearts." Remarkably, he wrote that statement more than one hundred years ago! What would he say if he were alive today? What would he say if he met you?

DOES MONEY HAVE ITS GRIP ON YOU?

To know whether your attitude about money and possessions is what it should be, ask yourself the following questions:

Am I preoccupied with things?

Am I envious of others?

Do I find my personal value in possessions?

Do I believe that money will make me happy?

Do I continually want more?

If you answered yes to one or more of those questions, you need to do some soul searching. Change your mindset. There's nothing wrong with possessing money or nice things. Likewise, there's nothing wrong with living modestly.

Materialism is a mindset. It affects the poor and rich alike.

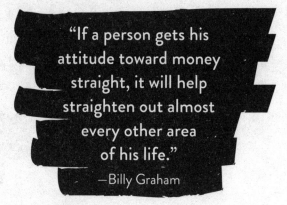

"If a person gets his attitude toward money straight, it will help straighten out almost every other area of his life."

—Billy Graham

MONEY WON'T MAKE YOU HAPPY

Even though most people would say they agree with the saying "Money won't buy happiness," they often still act like it's true. Thirty years ago, James Patterson and Peter Kim published the results of a national survey on morals in *The Day America Told the Truth*. They shared what percentage of people said they would perform a given action for ten million dollars.

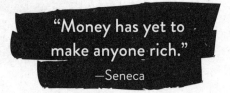

"Money has yet to make anyone rich."

—Seneca

Here is what they said:

> Abandon their entire family (25 percent)
> Become a prostitute for a week or longer (23 percent)
> Give up their American citizenship (16 percent)
> Leave their spouse (16 percent)
> Withhold testimony, letting a murderer go free (10 percent)
> Kill a stranger (7 percent)
> Put their children up for adoption (3 percent)

It's chilling how many people would destroy their lives and souls for money.

Both wealth and poverty only serve to amplify who you already are.

"Money doesn't change men,
it merely unmasks them.
If a man is naturally selfish,
or arrogant, or greedy,
the money brings it out;
that's all."

—Henry Ford

DEBT *WILL* MAKE YOU UNHAPPY

While possessing riches will never guarantee happiness or success, *owing* money can make you miserable.

If your outgo exceeds your income, then your upkeep will be your downfall. Solomon of ancient Israel was even more blunt. Summing up the condition of anyone in debt, he said, "The rich rule over the poor, and the borrower is slave to the lender." Who wants to be a slave, controlled by someone else?

FINANCIAL MARGIN WILL GIVE YOU OPTIONS

The bottom line is that money is nothing but a tool. Having money can help you achieve some goals. But its greatest worth is in its ability to give you choices.

If you have financial margin, you can own a more reliable car or repair the one you have if it breaks down. You may have the option to move if your place of work is far from you. You or your children might be able to attend a better school. You may be able to take off from work to attend your children's ball games or recitals. You can give to others. You may be able to change jobs to do something you love. Or take time off to volunteer.

All of these things are difficult to do if you're living
right up to—or beyond—your means.

**If you live from paycheck to paycheck,
you'll never be able to do anything but work.**

"ALL PROGRESS IS BASED UPON A UNIVERSAL INNATE DESIRE ON THE PART OF EVERY LIVING ORGANISM TO LIVE BEYOND ITS INCOME."

—Samuel Butler

EARN, MANAGE, GIVE

The only surefire way to have money is to earn it.
The best way to keep money is to manage it.

Working, earning, saving, and investing prepare you for the best of all things you can do with your money: giving.

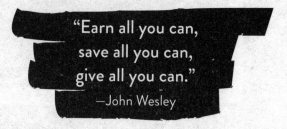

"Earn all you can,
save all you can,
give all you can."
—John Wesley

"The difference between the rich and the poor is that the rich invest their money and spend what's left, while the poor spend their money and invest what's left."

—Author unknown

"MONEY IS ANOTHER PAIR
OF HANDS TO HEAL AND FEED
AND BLESS THE DESPERATE
FAMILIES OF THE EARTH...
A MAN'S MONEY IS
AN EXTENSION OF HIMSELF."

—Bruce Larson

MAKE ROOM FOR FAITH

"I AM FULLY CONVINCED
THAT THE SOUL IS INDESTRUCTIBLE,
AND THAT ITS ACTIVITY
WILL CONTINUE THROUGH ETERNITY."

—Johann Wolfgang von Goethe

WHERE TO SEEK ANSWERS

There was a time when people hoped that science would provide all the answers to life's questions. But science cannot do that. Ironically, what is embraced as scientific fact changes from generation to generation. Consider the way the best scientists have looked at our solar system. Ptolemy believed the earth was at its center. Copernicus asserted that the sun was at its center and the planets moved around it in circular orbits. Kepler proved that the orbits were elliptical. Scientific belief continues to change based on additional information and understanding.

Contrast that with faith. The core beliefs of Judaism and Christianity have not changed in thousands of years. There is a spiritual aspect to human life that cannot be denied. Spiritual needs must be met spiritually. Nothing else will fill the void.

> "FAITH IS TO BELIEVE
> WHAT WE DO NOT SEE;
> AND THE REWARD OF THIS FAITH
> IS TO SEE WHAT WE BELIEVE."

—St. Augustine of Hippo

YOU ALREADY HAVE FAITH—WHERE DO YOU PUT IT?

Every day you act on beliefs that have little or no evidence to back them up.

That is also true in a spiritual sense. Just as one person has faith that God is real, an atheist has faith that God does not exist. Both people hold strong beliefs, and neither person can produce evidence to absolutely prove their point of view. Right now, you already have faith in something. Your goal should be to align your beliefs with whatever is true. Seek the truth, and you will find it.

LET UNCERTAINTY AND DIFFICULTY OPEN THE DOOR TO FAITH

Faith is not a sign of weakness. It is often an opportunity for a course correction in the journey of life. In a play by T. S. Eliot, one of his characters describes the uncertainty of the faith journey:

> The destination cannot be described; you will know very little until you get there; you will journey blind. But the way leads toward possession of what you have sought for in the wrong place.

If you are experiencing difficulties, explore faith in response to them.

Faith can not only help you through a crisis but also help you approach life with a whole new perspective afterward.

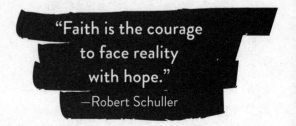

"Faith is the courage to face reality with hope."
—Robert Schuller

"[This] is the great conversation
in our life: to recognize and believe
that the many unexpected events
are not just disturbing interruptions
of our projects, but the way
in which God molds our hearts
and prepares us."

—Henri Nouwen

GIVE GOD A CHANCE

If you want to make room for faith, you must give God a chance. Let him into your life. No one else is worthy of our absolute and unconditional trust. James, one of the fathers of the first century church, advised, "Come near to God and he will come near to you."

> "Unbelief puts our circumstances between us and God. Faith puts God between us and our circumstances."
>
> —F. B. Meyer

AS GENUINE FAITH IS TESTED, IT DEEPENS

Faith gives peace and strength only if it's not superficial. The deeper the faith, the greater the potential it has to carry you through the rough times.

Perhaps nothing in recent history tested the faith of so many people so severely as the Holocaust. Viennese psychiatrist Viktor Frankl was one of the survivors of the Nazis' atrocities. From 1942 to 1945, he was imprisoned in four different concentration camps, including Auschwitz and Dachau. Frankl once said, "A weak faith is weakened by predicaments and catastrophes whereas a strong faith is strengthened by them."

Despite the horrors Frankl witnessed and the treatment he suffered, his faith got deeper.

"FAITH LIKE JOB'S
CANNOT BE SHAKEN BECAUSE
IT IS THE RESULT OF
HAVING BEEN SHAKEN."

—Abraham Heschel

"I prayed for faith, and thought that some day faith would come down and strike me like lightning. But faith did not seem to come. One day I read in the tenth chapter of Romans, 'Faith comes by hearing, and hearing by the word of God.' I had closed my Bible and prayed for faith. I now opened my Bible and began to study, and faith has been growing ever since."

—D. L. Moody

"WE ARE NOT HUMAN BEINGS
HAVING A SPIRITUAL EXPERIENCE.
WE ARE SPIRITUAL BEINGS
HAVING A HUMAN EXPERIENCE."

—Pierre Teilhard de Chardin

GIVE MORE THAN YOU TAKE

"NO MAN BECOMES RICH
UNLESS HE ENRICHES OTHERS."

—Andrew Carnegie

What is the greatest choice you can make to win at life? What value has a lasting impact? Being generous. When you give more than you take, you leave the world better than you found it.

Greatness is defined not by what you gain, but by what you give.

True generosity isn't a function of income—it begins with the heart. It's about serving others and looking for ways to add value to them. That's the way to achieve the greatest significance in your life.

"Life's most persistent and urgent question is, 'What are we doing for others?'"
—Martin Luther King Jr.

GENEROSITY IS ATTRACTIVE TO OTHERS

No one likes to be around people who think only of themselves. In contrast, nearly everyone enjoys being around people who give more than they take.

"How delightful is the company of
generous people, who overlook trifles
and keep their minds instinctively fixed on
whatever is good and positive in the world around
them. People of small caliber are always carping.
They are bent on showing their own superiority,
their knowledge or prowess or good breeding.
But magnanimous people have no vanity, they
have no jealousy, they have no reserves, and they
feed on the true and solid wherever they find it.
And what is more, they find it everywhere."

—Van Wyck Brooks

GENEROSITY TURNS YOUR FOCUS OUTWARD

Generosity can be described very simply as changing your focus from yourself to others. When you're occupied with giving to others and helping them succeed, it drives away selfishness.

Giving more than you take not only makes the world a better place but also makes the giver happier.

"NO MAN CAN LIVE HAPPILY
WHO REGARDS HIMSELF ALONE,
WHO TURNS EVERYTHING
TO HIS OWN ADVANTAGE.
YOU MUST LIVE FOR OTHERS
IF YOU WISH TO LIVE
FOR YOURSELF."

—Seneca

GENEROSITY ADDS VALUE TO OTHERS

One of the most significant things a person can do while on this earth is help others. Don't measure your life by the number of people who serve you or the amount of money you accumulate. **Look at how many people you serve.** The greater your giving, the greater you're living.

You never stand taller in the climb to success than when you bend down to help someone else up.

When you add value to others, you do not take anything away from yourself.

"You are not here merely to make a living. You are here in order to enable the world to live more amply, with greater vision, with a finer spirit of home and achievement. You are here to enrich the world, and you impoverish yourself if you forget the errand."

—Woodrow Wilson

GIVING HELPS THE GIVER

How do you feel when you do something for another person? Don't you feel a greater sense of purpose and pleasure for having done something right?

When you help others, you can't help but benefit.

You can't light another's path without casting light on your own.

"YOU HAVE NOT LIVED
A PERFECT DAY, EVEN THOUGH
YOU HAVE EARNED YOUR MONEY,
UNLESS YOU HAVE DONE SOMETHING
FOR SOMEONE WHO WILL NEVER
BE ABLE TO REPAY YOU."

—Ruth Smeltzer

"The world of the generous
gets larger and larger;
the world of the stingy
gets smaller and smaller.
The one who blesses others
is abundantly blessed;
those who help others are helped."

—King Solomon

DON'T WAIT FOR PROSPERITY TO GIVE

Your level of income and your desire to give have nothing to do with one another. Some of the most generous people in the world give from the little they have. Some of the stingiest have an abundance they hoard.

Generous people give not from the top of their purses, but from the bottom of their hearts. If you desire to become a more generous person, don't wait for your income to change. Change your heart. You do that by giving before you **feel** like it.

FIND WAYS TO GIVE EVERY DAY

Giving usually involves going out of your way, but you must keep your eyes open to find opportunities to give. Give help to those who need it. Be strategic about making a difference. Give to organizations you respect and trust. They're all around you.

"DO ALL THE GOOD YOU CAN,
TO ALL THE PEOPLE YOU CAN,
IN ALL THE WAYS YOU CAN,
AS LONG AS YOU CAN."

—D. L. Moody

LIVE YOUR

VALUE

CHOICES

TODAY

There are only a handful of important value choices you need to make in your entire lifetime to win at life. Most people overcomplicate life and get bogged down.

Make these twelve choices, and you will be successful:

- ☐ Focus on today.
- ☐ See the glass as half-full.
- ☐ View everyone as a potential friend.
- ☐ Do what you say you'll do.
- ☐ Put *important* ahead of *urgent*.
- ☐ Give your family your best.
- ☐ Make yourself better every day.
- ☐ Think your way to the top.
- ☐ Never put off your health.
- ☐ Keep money in perspective.
- ☐ Make room for faith.
- ☐ Give more than you take.

Once these choices have been made, all you have to do is get up each morning and determine to follow through with them today. Do that, and you will not only make the best of your day today, you will create the kind of tomorrow you desire.

Simple? Yes. Easy? Not always.
But it's a choice that's well within your reach.

ACKNOWLEDGMENTS

I want to say thank you to Charlie Wetzel and the rest of the team who assisted me with the formation and publication of this book. And to the people in my organizations who support it. You all add incredible value to me, which allows me to add value to others. Together, we're making a difference!